Becoming a

FIGURE SKATER

First published in the United States of America in 2004
by UNIVERSE PUBLISHING
A Division of Rizzoli International Publications, Inc.
300 Park Avenue South
New York, NY 10010
www.rizzoliusa.com

© 2004 Nancy Ellison
Foreword by Sasha Cohen
Introduction by Craig Maurizi
Design by Opto Design

2004 2005 2006 2007/ 10 9 8 7 6 5 4 3 2 1

Printed in the United States

ISBN: 0-7893-1189-5

Library of Congress Control Number: 2004110347

Becoming a

FIGURE SKATER

NANCY ELLISON

INTRODUCTION BY CRAIG MAURIZI

FOREWORD BY SASHA COHEN

UNIVERSE

For Bill, my love,
and for Wilha May Duncan...
Welcome to life!

Foreword

BY SASHA COHEN

Foreword

BY SASHA COHEN

I remember my first competition. The rink was freezing, the smell was musty—I could smell the hairspray securing my painfully tight bun, and taste the lipstick. I was nervous. Very nervous. I got on the ice and did the routine I had been practicing with my coach for months. I didn't do it perfectly, but I tried my best and was happy with my efforts. My family, friends, and I went out to a diner in the neighborhood afterwards and ate and laughed and talked. It ended up being a really nice evening.

That was an important night for me. I worked hard to prepare, I did my best, and afterwards, I relaxed and enjoyed myself. I think that night taught me a lot about what becoming an ice skater would be like. There's no question—skating competitively is a lot of work. My schedule varies depending on where I'm competing and what the event is, but nearly every day I'm on the ice for three hours, and training off the ice for another three. And the next day, I get up and do the same thing again. I love it—love the competing, love the travel—there's nothing I would rather be doing. But there are certain challenges to the sport.

Staying positive is one of those challenges. There's a lot—a lot—of falling down and getting back up in skating. There's learning new moves, like combinations and triple jumps, that require a lot of work and perseverance to master. And then there's stringing together those jumps and turns and choreography to make a routine. Four minutes is how long my free program lasts. Just four minutes to show the world how I've practiced all my life for this moment. I've done these four minutes over and over and can do them perfectly in rehearsal, but sometimes I get out there and it just doesn't go the way I wanted it to. And that's skating: You get back up and you keep going. You keep going until the next time.

That special time when it does go right. That's the moment I've been practicing for. That feeling of accomplishment and pure joy are what continue to drive me every day.

I've now been a skater for most of my life, which is something I am very proud of. So much has changed from those early days of skating: The stakes are a lot different for me now than when I was seven. The competitions are huge, the seats are packed, and I'm skating against the best in the world. There are camera crews, reporters, and interviews afterward. But the same spirit from that first competition is still in me. I still get nervous. I still train hard, go out there and give it my all.

And afterwards, I still unwind with my family and friends. When it's over, I take a short break and then get back into training. It's back on the ice with my coach and time to practice. Because—just like when I was seven—I continue to love the wind on my face and every challenge that the sport brings. I love being a skater.

9

Introduction

BY CRAIG MAURIZI

Introduction

BY CRAIG MAURIZI

Figure skating stirs up love and passion. Must be something about the sensation of gliding, of feeling the wind in your hair. Or perhaps it's the sparkling dresses worn during competitions, the thrill of competing in front of a crowd and landing that jump, executing the perfect turn.

Regardless of where it comes from, skating—becoming a skater—means loving the sport from the beginning and loving it through the hard work, bad days, and disappointments. The passion for the ice must be present to master a new maneuver, to practice day in and day out the same routine until it's nailed. For it is love, passion, but just as importantly, perseverance and determination, that makes a champion.

I've been a skating coach for much of my life. I'm there on the ice every day–I come to work in warm clothes and spend my time with young hopefuls. I love it. It's cold and tiring and can be frustrating and exhausting, but being surrounded by such drive and strong will–there's nothing I would rather be doing.

To train a champion is, well, amazing. I'm still in awe of Tara Lipinski, who I helped to ready for her 1998 Olympic victory. What sticks out most from my time with Tara is her incredible consistency. I have never in my life witnessed a skater who could skate a program that included seven triple jumps perfectly. Literally: Almost every training day in her life she would come in and do that routine flawlessly. If you're a coach or skater you can really understand the enormity of this. It was as though failing wasn't an option. She was so confident in her ability to train at this level on a daily basis (which she did) that on the rare occasion it didn't happen she became almost mystified at her mistake.

Tara, perhaps, more than anyone I've trained, epitomized the mindset of a champion. Every morning, she arrived at the rink at

8 a.m. to warm up. At around 9 she would get on the ice and warm up for her long program. No stopping. Then she would break and do her short routine. Again, no stopping, and if anything was not going exactly right we would spend the rest of the morning working on those things. If things went well she would work on new tricks to put into the program like triple lutz-triple loop combinations or new spins. After the intense morning training Tara worked one hour (either on or off the ice) with a ballet specialist. Break time was from 11:45am to 1:15pm. The afternoon training was a mirror image of the morning training. Since Tara was home-schooled she would have to go home around 3:00 pm and do four hours of schooling before going to bed. The difference in what Tara did and others did not was she approached each session on each day with an unrivaled determination to make that day the best she could. She made use of every bit of her training

14

time. She didn't talk on the ice, she was never late for a session, and took direction from her coaches with no complaints. And she loved the sport. She's a skating champion, in every way.

———

Sometimes, one mistake can make the difference between taking first place and taking second place. And it simply comes down to pure luck.

Of course, great skaters can make a lot of their own luck. The skater who can exhibit the mental toughness and focus for an entire program will undoubtedly be on top some of the time. But what is a "great skater?" And how do you describe a champion? The term champion takes more forms than the obvious one of a person standing at the top of a podium. In my mind, a champion is a skater who has passion, drive, and talent. This is the only way to determine whether a skater is a champion or not. And if you happen to stand at the top of a medal podium someday, then it's icing on the cake—nothing more. You're setting yourself up for failure if winning first place is your only motivation. Why? Because there are countless factors that can prevent this from happening. Maybe you get sick the day of competition or you step on cement right before your performance and your blade can't glide well or you miss a jump in your program you land almost all the time. If you're a champion, you know it. And you don't need to take gold to prove it.

Skating competitively is about so much more than winning. Becoming a skater is a journey—it doesn't come down to one victory, one event, one competition. It's about that sense of satisfaction when you master something difficult. It's about feeling great the first time you land a jump or perfect a turn or get through your whole routine without falling. It takes incredibly hard work and sticking to your goals. You'll get there.

Skating should be about having fun. It should be about the excitement of learning new things and making new friends. The desire or need to win is way down on the list. I don't mean that striving to win isn't important—it is!—but it's more important to focus on that joy, that fun. Joy is something that every skater needs to feel from the first time they go on the ice and every day of their lives that they're training and working to get better.

Competitions can be exciting challenges where you can learn

a lot about yourself and grow as a person. They can also be scary, emotionally draining times in a skater's life. The key to a rewarding competition is preparation.

A specific daily routine is laid out within a specific time frame with specific expectations for the training on a daily or weekly basis. The skater must understand that the expectations (which should be challenging but not impossible) must be met within the time frames they have been given. When these expectations are met the skater derives an inner confidence within themselves. By adhering to the preparation guidelines the skater takes to the ice for competition with huge confidence in their ability to skate a personal best because they have done it in practice many times. Doing all your preparation correctly will ensure that the chance for competing well is higher but nothing is ever guaranteed in sports. Assuming the preparation has been excellent you then look to the personality of the skater to give you more of a sense of how well they will perform. The three factors—passion, drive and talent (both physical and mental)—will help the skater place higher or lower. The first two factors enable the preparation process to go better than expected or not as well as you had hoped for. The talent plays a role here but passion and drive can overcome less talent but more talent can never overcome the lack of passion and drive. I think a skater can be taught some of these characteristics but only to a certain degree. Giving the skater training guidelines and making them stick to them produces discipline and a higher sense of confidence. If the coach loves what they are doing and expresses his/her passion for skating, the skater will undoubtedly learn to enjoy skating more. The skaters who excel the most have these qualities built into them. They are not taught. They ask to come to the rink every day. They need to accomplish the daily tasks their coach has set for them and are undaunted in their quest for excellence even on a bad day.

This book will take you through the nuts and bolts of how to become a figure skater. It provides you with the necessary information you need to give you a direction in how to get started on the path in this exciting and challenging sport. But ultimately, this book is about having fun. And that's what skating is really about.

19

Discovering

DISCOVERING

Getting on the ice that first time is so scary! It's really hard not to wobble around a lot. My brother, Robby, and I held onto each other tightly that first time—we were both afraid to fall down!

But then it started to be fun:
It feels so free! We both
loved the wind on our faces
(though it was so cold!).

26

Robby skated off—fast. He fell (over and over) but he got back up and really let it rip. He was practically flying across the rink. I think he'll be an amazing hockey player one day.

As for me, I was a little clumsy at first. Keeping one leg in the air is much harder than it looks. But I kept at it, skating around the ice until I felt more comfortable and confident.

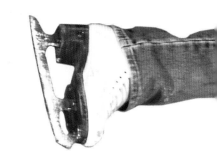

That day, I fell in love with the ice. I never wanted to stop! I decided right then that I wanted to become a figure skater.

Getting Ready

Before you start skating lessons, you need to prepare. It's too much work to go from your skates to your shoes and then back to your skates, so it's important to have a pair of skate guards so that you don't ruin the floors—or more importantly, your blades!

Wearing big sweatshirts and jeans is okay if you're going to skate for fun on an outdoor pond, but in a skating rink you need to wear fitted gear so that your teacher can make sure you're skating correctly. It can be chilly, however, so I always have a warm fleece jacket with me. Once you start skating, you usually warm up pretty quickly—skating is great exercise! Also, make sure that if you have long hair, it's pulled back. I keep mine short so that I don't ever have to worry about it getting in the way!

37

Starting Out

During your first lessons, the most important thing is learning how to feel confident on the ice. Our teacher had us use these cones so that we could learn about balance (and so that we would be brave enough to let go of the wall!).

The next thing that you will
learn is how to fall. Nope,
I'm not kidding! Learning
how to fall the right way is
one of the most important
things you can learn in
skating lessons. If you know
how to fall it not only makes
falling less scary, but it also
prevents injuries.

42

Of course, learning how to
stop is just as essential. It's
tough at first—you have to put
one skate in front of the other
to come to a complete stop.

Once you master balance,
falling, and stopping, it
feels like you can do almost
anything on the ice!

BECOMING A FIGURE SKATER

Getting Serious

Skating quickly became my passion. I wanted to be doing it all the time. When my parents realized that I was very serious about skating, I started training with Sara and Neil Rubin, my coaches. I went for private lessons twice a week. It was in private lessons that I started working on things like turns and jumps.

Here I'm working on a spiral turn, which is almost like an arabesque in ballet. Sara is showing me how to keep my shoulders back and my arms out. She's also reminding me to lock my bottom knee.

This is a layback spin. Sara is telling my to loosen my arms more—it's really important in layback spins to have your arms shaped like they're holding a beach ball.

49

50

Sara is really great about showing me what she wants and then helping me get in the right position. While I practice this spiral, Sara is reminding me to arch my back and keep my chin up.

When your back is arched
and your chin is up, it
makes every move look
more graceful. It also gives
the move more power and
shows your enthusiasm.

This is a tough one. It's called a catch layback spin. A regular layback spin is one of the loveliest spins. You execute it on one foot while your body bends straight back from your waist and your arms are over your head. When you do the catch layback, you grab your blade. It's really important to grab your blade at a right angle— otherwise, you could really hurt yourself. The reason I like to do catch layback spins is because you can spin even faster than you do on a regular layback spin.

BECOMING A FIGURE SKATER

This is called "shoot-the-duck." Isn't that a funny name? This is something that beginning skaters learn because it helps with the balance that you need later for sit spins. When you do a shoot-the-duck, you bend as low as you can on your skating knee and you push your other leg in front of you. Your back should stay straight, your head should be up, and you press your hands forward for support.

Once you can do shoot-the-duck, you can start to learn a sit spin. Here I am getting into a good low position, trying to get my back really straight but bending forward in about a 60-degree angle toward my free leg. My foot is turned out.

Here I'm exiting the spin. I lean forward while I bring my free leg around in a circular motion and stand up on my skating leg. When you finish, you should hold it for a moment or two to show that you have balance and control.

57

Sara and I are always working on making my leg go higher. It's much prettier if your leg is high up. She always reminds me to keep my head up, up, up!

Advanced Training

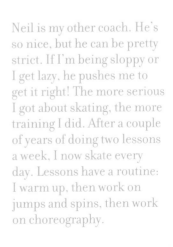

Neil is my other coach. He's so nice, but he can be pretty strict. If I'm being sloppy or I get lazy, he pushes me to get it right! The more serious I got about skating, the more training I did. After a couple of years of doing two lessons a week, I now skate every day. Lessons have a routine: I warm up, then work on jumps and spins, then work on choreography.

Here I am warming up,
doing some crossovers, and
then stretching out my leg.
It's very important to warm
out your body before doing
any jumps or spins.

64

65

67

Falling is a part of everyday training. Here I am trying to do a sit spin that's low enough. I got too low and I couldn't get back up! Neil doesn't ever let me give up, though. When you fall, you just get right back up and try it again.

BECOMING A FIGURE SKATER

I love doing choreography. Once you start competing, your coach picks some music and you learn some dance moves to do at competition. My choreography features Irish step dancing. It only took one lesson for me to learn it. but to get it perfectly takes a long time. The trick to my dance is that I go across the ice at an angle. rather than straight across.

Training is hard work!
I love it though.

Performance

The jumps you need to
know in order to compete
are called loop, toe loop,
Salchow, lutz, flip, and the
hardest, the axel. The axel
jumps are the hardest
because there are one-and-
a-half rotations—not just
one, like the other jumps.
To do it right, you need to
gather a lot of momentum
at the beginning. That's
what I'm doing here.

I spend a lot of time
practicing my axel jump.
I try to get as high as I can.

76

Nailed it!

78

Of course, the way you spin is also a big deal in performance and competition. It's important to look graceful, like a ballerina, when you spin. That's why Sara and Neil are always reminding me to arch my back and keep my head back.

The layback spin, like the one I'm doing here, should finish with what's called a forward scratch spin. That's when you take your free foot and cross it over your skating foot so that it rests on the outside of your skating ankle and pull your arms in toward your body. This can make you go incredibly fast and really adds a flourish to the end of any of your spins. It looks like you're flying!

Competition

Competitions—especially the big ones—make me nervous.

I know a lot of girls might be better than I am, but I have to keep a positive attitude.

Coach usually tells me to do my best right
before I go on: Hold your head high. he says.

Keep your hands pressed—when they're sloppy they
look like puppy dog paws. That always makes me laugh.

To go with my Irish step
dance, I got a bright green
costume. After your coach
picks out your music and
you know what the theme is,
you go to a designer and tell
them the idea. I love my
costume! It's my favorite.

Once I'm out on the ice, I
usually stop feeling nervous
and start to feel excited. It's
so amazing to hear everybody
cheering you on!

Here's where all that time
practicing pays off. I know
my routine perfectly
because I've done it so
many times. Head up, back
straight, shoulders back . . .

BECOMING A FIGURE SKATER

Is it over already?

Time to take a bow.

Ta da! I did my best, and I had fun doing it. That's all that matters to me. Maybe someday there will be nationals — or even the Olympics—I think that if you work hard and you love what you do, you can do anything you set your mind to. I love being a figure skater!

I would like to thank Shannon Tarleton, our enchanting skater, for the charm and skills that she brought to this book. Not only are you a talented skater, but you were simply a pleasure to work with—I hope that all of your dreams come true. I am also grateful to Shannon's wonderful, generous family: Robert, Ann Marie, and Robby; we couldn't have done this without you! (Especially Robby, who I'm sure we'll see playing professional hockey someday soon.)

ACKNOWLEDGMENTS

Thank you to my editor Holly Rothman, who did so much to bring this book together, and to my publisher Charles Miers for his support. Also thanks to the production team at Rizzoli for their enthusiasm and energy and Opto Design's John Klotnia and Sandy Zimmerman for designing such a lovely book.

I thank my assistants, Ken Ferdman and Walter Murdock, for their digital expertise and camera assistance and Lisa Poulos and Angela Titolo for their help in production.

Finally, thank you to Sasha Cohen for her inspiring foreword and Craig Maurizi for his engaging and insightful introduction.

— Nancy Ellison

95